NOCTURNE
NEW AND SELECTED POEMS

by Mike Dillon

For information contact:

Unsolicited Press

Portland, Oregon

www.unsolicitedpress.com

orders@unsolicitedpress.com

619-354-8005

Book Design: Kathryn Gerhardt

Editor: Summer Stewart

ISBN: 978-1-963115-09-3

Acknowledgments

Various selections in the "New Poems" section were published in journals in print and online:

Ekstasis Magazine: Ars Poetica

Poetry Scotland: There

The Galway Review: Death of a Nature Writer, Cold Water Swimming, Eurydice Update, Boys on the Dock

Alba: Borderlands

Bellowing Ark: A Black and White Photograph in a History Book

Ekphrastic Review: Nocturne in Blue and Gold: Old Battersea Bridge

Shot Glass Journal: Self Portrait in Charcoal

Poetica Review: What the Tribal Elder Told Me

Minotaur: World War I: Future Nobel Laureate Eugenio Montale Finds His Calling

"Selected Poems" were drawn from the following books:

Riverbank, Bellowing Ark Press, 2003

the road behind, Red Moon Press, 2003

That Which We Have Named, Bellowing Ark Press, 2008

Coracle, Bellowing Ark Press, 2011

As We Are Known, Bellowing Ark Press, 2014

contingencies, Red Moon Press, 2014

Outside the Garden, Red Moon Press, 2017

Departures: Poetry and Prose on the Removal of Bainbridge Island's Japanese Americans After Pearl Harbor, Unsolicited Press, 2019.

Suquamish and Other Poems, Bellowing Ark Press, 2019

The Return, Finishing Line Press, 2021

Close Enough, Finishing Line Press, 2023

Introduction

Gathered here is a selection culled from all of my books: six books of poetry, three books of haiku, and two recent chapbooks, *The Return* and *Close Enough*. About a quarter of my book-published poems made the cut.

My gratitude goes out to Summer and the team at Unsolicited Press for making *Nocturne* possible. They are passionate, deeply informed makers of books that matter. And a pleasure to work with.

My first book, *Riverbank*, was published by Bellowing Ark Press in 2003, the same year Red Moon Press brought out my first book of haiku, *the road behind*.

Bellowing Ark journal began publishing my poems in the early 1990s. Robert Ward, who died in 2019, was the mastermind behind the journal and press. An established curmudgeon, Robert was also generous, brilliant, and committed to the poetry he believed in. He had no time for the narcissism of poetic despair. The search for beauty is difficult, he allowed, but redemptive. I like to think William Blake was the first to clasp Robert's hand on the other side of the river.

My haiku appeared in various haiku magazines for fifteen years in this country and overseas, before Red Moon Press brought out *the road behind*, which has undergone a second printing. My deep gratitude goes to Jim Kacian at the press for believing in my work.

A word about *Departures: Poetry and Prose on the Removal of Bainbridge Island's Japanese Americans After Pearl Harbor*, published by Unsolicited Press in 2019.

The best account of what happened on Bainbridge Island is Mary Woodward's book about her parents: *In Defense of Our Neighbors: The Walt and Milly Woodward Story*. Those who find themselves on Bainbridge Island, where I grew up, would do well to visit the Japanese American Exclusion Memorial there. The

Woodwards, young, shallow-pocketed publishers of the *Bainbridge Review* on that December Day in 1941, are historical proof of what a difference a principled stand can make in a small community. Their nearby presence was a north star in my firmament as I grew up; their heroic example was one of the reasons I felt called to publish community newspapers.

I started writing *Departures* after a lifetime of unknowingly preparing to do it. The parents of some of my best friends had been in the camps. The rise of Trumpism was my wake-up call to write about what happened from my own, post-War vantage point.

In March 2023 I gave a forty-minute talk at the Keats-Shelley House in Rome on "The Holiness of the Heart's Affections: The Courage and Modernity of John Keats," in which I focused on Keats's statement in one of his extraordinary letters: "That which is creative must create itself."

Keats, without thinking about it in these terms, was an early 19th century avatar of the "existence before essence" school; he would have been right at home on the Left Bank in the 1950s. And yet, in his strenuous walking tour in the north of England and Scotland in 1818, which likely hastened his early death, Keats carried a copy of Henry Francis Cary's translation of *The Divine Comedy* in his rucksack. Dante, in Western Christendom, is the Babe Ruth of the "essence before existence" school.

The tug between those poles has played out in my poetry: faith and doubt, the desire to adore and the need to curse. In the end, though, for me, it's not a fifty-fifty proposition: I don't want to live in a world, or poetic universe, where the word "transubstantiation" has walked the plank.

As for the rest: I've made no mention of awards, or award nominations, or the smattering of positive reviews my work has received. I can only refer to a friend's email ten days before she died: "I read your poems in bed before falling asleep. They take me places I cherish in the night."

This is sufficient. The rest is silence. Or ought to be.

Table of Contents

from *That Which We Have Named (2008)*

from *Coracle (2011)*

from *As We Are Known (2014)*

from the sequence *Fidelities*

from the sequence Suquamish

Haiku

from The Return (2021)

from Close Enough

To Gus, Rosie and Hazel

In the midst of winter, I found there was, within me, an invincible summer.

Albert Camus

NOCTURNE
NEW AND SELECTED POEMS

New Poems

Third Grade

The question on the chalkboard
was no question at all.
Our teacher had the sing-song answer
cocked and loaded behind her back.
And so, we sang it. We all sang along.

And so, the guillotine dropped
on the coin of light shining
at the far end of the penumbral,
cranial corridors under construction
in so many young minds
the way an eyelid shuts.

And something inside me
dropped one floor.
And for certain others, I fear,
more than one floor.

Ars Poetica

He deconstructs his poems
into shattered churches.
He wants to stand astride
a fresh pile of written rubble
and rub death into his eyes
where roses should blow.
As for churches: a void trapped
in stone, he says. That's all.
He is deaf to the echoing whisper
in the empty nave: "Be not afraid."
And he is sore afraid,
whose poems are born of his flinching
to the sound of crashing glass and stone.
He writes it all down, how he mines and assays
each twitch of his exposed, wind-chafed
nerves wriggling in the mirror
for the lack of the love they seek
as he dresses himself each morning
in the shroud of his poetic dolor.
Elsewhere, roses blow in the light.

There

A quiet place. A winter afterthought.
Traces of a path through the brush follow
a creek into a bare stand of alders.
Serrated crow caws fill the four corners.
A pewter gob of sun lightens the ashen sky,
the iridescence of moss. The way here
crosses three mud-squdged fields.
No boot prints precede you.
No Keep Out signs are needed.
The land keeps its own counsel. A quiet,
subordinate place, the way a life turns out
to be less than it might have been.

The vague path skirts a wide estuary,
its enigmatic mix of fresh and salt water.
The breeze off the sound ticks through the sedge,
the stone-gray waters a glitter of light
opening out to distant ocean.
Rotted pilings. Gull scritch.
A grey heron wades the slack tide.
You've come here again

with your dream of egress instead

of the place where you are expected.

Here, the past is a little easier to rearrange

for as long as you keep the path

that brought you here at your back.

Borderlands

Thin as a knife blade
slipped between a peach
and its skin are their differences.
But a knife blade just the same.

Death of a Nature Writer

In his last days they carried objects from the river
up to the house and placed them beneath his bed.

A bald eagle's feather.
A cottonwood branch.
An owl pellet: all minced fur and bones.
A blue stone.
A mole's skull.
A crow's crow-black feather.
A maple leaf, mostly brown.
A bear turd, hard as stone.
A jar half-full of the river's stilled water.

They brought these things, bearing a green silence.
It was August. The river was low.

When the visions came no one was surprised.
All kinds of new friends flew about the room.
He called to them with wide open eyes.

After two months without rain,
the first of three days of rain drummed the roof.

"He's happy," his brother said.

On the third morning, as the river rose
and the rain softened to a stop,
his eyes closed.

Cold Water Swimming

There's a place where the dream inside this one
flashes before it vanishes quicker than a serpent's tail.
Quick enough it might have something to do with eternity.

It's there when I dive into the cold sea,
tiny as Blake's translucent grain of sand in Lambeth,
cryptic as a note from God slipped under the door.

I mean that evanescent moment
between the cold water's whoosh past my ears
and the arctic thunder in my marrow.

It's there and then not there in this world,
scant as the moment must be between a stopped heart
and the knowledge of it —

a blue sky glimpsed in a breath span
where a white dove bears the long-lost plans
for a legendary cathedral still waiting to be built.

A moment to make the prophets stammer.

A moment as beautiful as earth might be

before the cold pours in.

A Black and White Photograph in a History Book

The March afternoon sun sifts through the old cedar
and bathes three Dutch irises *en pointe*

in a white vase beside the southern window.
A book of long ago and far away sprawls in your lap.

The photograph evinces a slight wind:
A row of poplars, descended from Monet,

flash their trout-like, Mozartian leaves beside
the smooth river rolling its barber poles of light.

The white cloud in the upper right corner,
Botticelli-round, would be moving.

In the foreground: a long line of people emptied
from the village with one suitcase each, the caption says.

They wait for the trucks, wait forever in the present tense,
hedged in by the familiar, square-cut helmets.

It is still early in the War. Even so,

there is no mistaking the taut apprehension

shadowing the faces innocent of our own three a.m. knowledge.

Sooner than later, the white cloud will have moved on.

The quay will be empty, the river flowing past

the poplars still flashing in the wind.

The sun has moved south, off the three irises.

You turn the page that won't be turned.

Eurydice Update

The view to the west is fine.

A flashing stream needles

through a windless grove of cottonwoods

past a village's red tile roofs

in the valley below

where swallows loop and tease a spire,

the orchard foams white with blossoms.

A wafer moon floats overhead.

An owl, pillowed trumpet,

announces itself from the woods.

Four in the afternoon.

The time when the day drifts

towards the promissory gentleness

of the far, blue mountains.

One hundred yards below

she takes in the scene, her back turned to him.

When he calls, she doesn't move.

He calls again.

She doesn't move.

Then she slowly turns her head

to cage him in the moment

where he will be

forever left behind.

Nocturne in Blue and Gold: Old Battersea Bridge, by James Abbot McNeill Whistler, c. 1872-75.

Smudged blues and blacks with streaks of fireworks in the distance.

Whistler's Japonisme phase: a flat, calligraphic impressionism where the first lights of dusk stipple the city.

In the foreground, a dark stanchion from below meets the bridge's dark horizontal over the darkening Thames. Intersecting shadows that form a kind of surreal **T**. Or, if you squint — a Cross, though no Cross, as far as we know, disturbed Whistler's sleep. Yet a first or last glance confirms it: a Cross is there.

Maybe it's just one of those Freudian, accidental truths. Or maybe the Cross — intersection of time and eternity, redemption through pain — is embedded pretty much everywhere we look.

"The one characteristic of a beautiful form is that one can put into it whatever one wishes, and see in it whatever one chooses to see," wrote Whistler's friend Oscar Wilde.

Shadowy, silhouetted lives walk across the bridge. Or the top of the Cross. They can't see the figure hunched on a pier far below. The urban loneliness of Eliot's "unreal city," fifty or so years in the future, is already here.

We've all been those people walking across a bridge, under the gaze of someone's appraising eye, like our own gazing at this picture in a book. And somewhere, we've surely seen that indistinct man hunched on the pier far below, fallen through a crack in his life, whose anonymous features will remain vividly whatever they are beneath an un-lifted sheet in a city morgue.

Prow to wave, the rest of us keep moving.

Self-Portrait in Charcoal, by Käthe Kollwitz (German) 1934

Behold what time

and the times have done.

Behold this face

worn as an old mountain.

They gave us a war

and it took my son.

It will come around again.

Remember: mountains don't break.

Give me your hand.

Look into these eyes.

Do not look away.

Especially at the end.

Käthe Kollwitz (1867-1945), who lost her youngest son in World War I, was the great German artist of social realism and the grief of war.

What the Tribal Elder Told Me

Sometimes I dream of *swah'netk'qhu*
and the hot summer nights when the rush
of its waters past my bedroom window
carried me deep into sleep.

Then came two white men
on black horses who rode our brown hills.
They measured our world through strange instruments.
They measured and wrote things down.

My brother and I ran to tell our parents.
This was ten years before the dam flooded our town.
On that day my people, along with rattlesnake and coyote,
took to the brown hills.

Now our river is a dead lake.
The white man from the green side of the mountains
comes here and sees only a sunny playground
for his two weeks paid vacation.

Some nights I still dream of hearing quick waters

flow past my bedroom window.

When I awake into day I remember:

A dead lake is silent. But not in the dream.

swah'netk'qhu is one of the Native American names for the Columbia River.

The great dam is Grand Coulee Dam in Washington State, finished in 1942.

World War I: Future Nobel Laureate Eugenio Montale Finds His Calling

Almost dawn. Time for the twenty-year-old future poet
to return to his lines with his night patrol.

Three Austrian soldiers stumble out of the shadows.

They stand there as shadows themselves — and drop their rifles
when they grasp the odds.

It would be easier for the night patrol to shoot the three of them
except the noise would draw their brethren.

Montale fishes into a shadow's bulging pocket.
He withdraws a worn volume of Rilke.

The shadow doesn't move. Montale's eyes move from the book
to the shadow. This time he sees the shadow's face.

A face that gazes back.

Boys on the Dock

*Nicht ärgern, nur wundern

I've watched those three boys grow
into their thirteen-year-old selves —
cold water swimmers, baseball players,
deft fly fishers.

Now I watch them set aside the undersized
Dungeness crabs from their pot
and execute a booted St. Vitus stomp
of shell crack and gruel spurt
until I yell stop! They do, like shot birds.

And they drift back toward their old selves.
And the four of us stand there in hushed wonder
as the glints and flashes fade from transgression's
underground stream.

*Don't be angry. Just admire.
A wooden sign hung over the portal to a destroyed church
in Belgium in the early days of World War I.

In Medias Res

Now you have come

to a fresh spring

where two paths meet

on a cliff above the sea

as dawn seeps through

that deep-down crack inside you

with just enough light

for you to find the way

to the crease in the map.

from Riverbank *(2003)*

Letter to My Sister

From the early 1990s

What, beyond the third day of rain
falling and still falling upon our family reunion
made you excuse yourself,
go striding toward the kitchen
(More beer for great-uncle rainwater eyes, you sighed)
and keep on going?
And so, you became your letters:
from the Peace Corps in Africa,
then teacher of the migrants in the Sacramento Delta,
and now, from San Francisco,
a nurse for young men in a hospice.

I read your letters over and over
and try hard not to presume anything
about your travels or your life alone
in a city apartment cloaked by the American night.
I try not to presume anything, my sister,
not even that the strong columns I always knew
were there inside you remain unbroken.

Even so, they seem unbroken.

I get this from your stray vignettes:

how one left you his bedside book

of *Japanese Death Poems* and how, the night he died,

his parents took you to their hotel for dinner,

the kid sister who came up to bat long ago

and took her stance in the dusk.

The neighborhood boys backed up.

I led off from second, secretly proud,

knowing I would soon be home.

High in a dark fir, the last robin caroled.

Higher still, the first star was there,

tiny and patient as a childhood memory.

Vigils

Because I have seen God face to face,
he said, yet my life has been spared
— Genesis

When you turned out the light you thought

just another bad night's sleep ahead.

And at first you slept until a doubled fist

dug into your hip socket and pain,

trout-belly white, flashed from the deeps.

The fight was on with something mulish,

something heavier than the midnight stone

that squeezes your breath into the hovering ghosts

of those things you did long ago.

All night you two wrestled until the dawn-robin caroled,

a strange voice croaked: "Let me go."

And it was your voice, sure as rifle crack,

you heard declare: "Not until you bless me."

You rise from the empty, storm-tossed bed.

You draw back the yellowed curtain,

your mind clear as blue sky after a week of rain.

Out the window, more rain.

Dried blood throbs beneath your nails.

Out on the sidewalk, you notice you are limping.

You look around and see others, too,

are limping. Some more. Some less.

Like a child you want to call out to them

but instead keep silent as they thread

their ways through the rain

with the mysterious blessedness of the wounded.

Walking on. Walking. Just like you.

Meuse-Argonne: 1956

Out the window April rain fell upon moss
through the salal and cedar-lit afternoon.

My six-year-old life sat at the sill and opened
the music box to a tinkling waltz of forest & court.

My mother and grandfather talked on in the kitchen
where grandfather, tall as Lincoln, gaunt as a legal argument,

spoke of long-ago, muddy roads that never dried,
of moving up to a place called Meuse-Argonne,

of how he had lied about his age to be with his brother.
I closed the music box.

"We rushed them across a big field.
He fell beside me. I had to keep moving."

Someone was weeping. They talked in whispers.
April rain fell on the strange words Meuse-Argonne.

Starter Home

Our first baby tucked under arm we ducked
through the looking-glass gate
set in a high laurel hedge and emerged
to face a mossed, swayback roofline
and a realtor standing beneath spring-white clouds
sugar-coating the lack of square footage.

She opened the door: nothing was straight.
Roll a ball upon this old fir floor, I declared,
and it'll come back eventually.
The realtor coughed. My eyes darted to my wife's.
We knew we would take it without discussing,
ever again, square footage.

And so, we came to live in a place
settled and worn like the face of someone
who'd lived a life worth living. Just an old spinster,
a villager whispered, who kept to herself
and played piano late into the night.
Ah, so much depth in so little square footage.

More years passed, but still in back:
the soft vocables of a quick stream
and the perfection of a pine I thought
possible only in the mind of Basho,
and her flowers still arising in spring
heedless of anyone's square footage.

Now our two boys are in their teens,
who have helped our small house
shape itself around them. And what the hell:
They've grown to know love is round, not square,
here where we know the names of the stars
passing overhead and laughter at dinner.
And never, not once, have they asked about square footage.

Contingencies

After the dinner party talk of Rome

featuring someone's funny story about a taxi;

after talk of Van Gogh, the Sixties, fly fishing,

the People Magazining of Montana,

the talk arrives at Hiroshima. Meaning:

we'd uncorked plenty of wine with more waiting.

The community college history teacher across from me

says Lincoln would have dropped the first bomb

but never the second, igniting protests all around.

Our lawyer host beams: he imagines himself

as some kind of keeper of a smart salon.

I take another swallow of Macon Blanc

and continue to shut up. Macon Blanc:

A connoisseur might sniff, swirl and smack

while fondly recalling the Valley of the Rhone

but if my dad were in this room

I know what he'd remember in silence —

his march up that valley in December 1944,

a right turn toward the Rhine in a record-cold winter.

A lucky leg bullet subtracted him

from the universe of sudden death.

When peace came in May he unsealed fresh orders:

Japan. Like Keats coughing up blood, a death warrant.

The two bombs of August sent him home.

And the dinner party talk drones on,

our host beaming over his lively table.

As for me, shards of an old nightmare flash.

A girl's silhouette printed upon a crumbling wall.

Thirsty silhouettes bent to the thickening river Ota.

I take another swig of Macon Blanc.

Point, counterpoint go on. And on.

My shy tongue touches my two front teeth,

proof that I am still here. Just to make sure.

At Least Once Each November 22

I remember eighth grade stripped of Whitman's lilacs
and the sudden buses to take us home
idling outside as my best friend cried

beside his locker and begged me not to tell
while I stood inside a secret thicket
where a strange white wind beat the leaves.

Ever since, before something bad might happen—
that pause, once, when our child's doctor
cleared his throat, or before I give a wrong answer

even still, the white wind might arise, as it does
each time that far November is replayed,
the blue motorcade turning toward us

in that grainy, morning-bright film. Watch,
this is history, intones an older voice in the room
and I watch like a good boy again

the last of the sunlit face before it changes.

And no one hears the wind beating louder, louder —

and then it happens. The rest of my life begins.

Once

In back of the shed I adjusted my elbows
to dad's uneven fence and let my shooting eye
sight down the black barrel of my BB gun
where a black-capped chickadee, tiny acrobat,
flitted from branch to budding branch.

A twitch of my trigger finger would carve
another notch on my gun butt, recording, once again,
how some kinds of innocence drop
plumb to the ground faster
than feathers drifting down.

My twelve-year-old hunter's blood up,
I tracked the bird in sunlight,
its mud-dark eyes bright as planets
before something broke inside
and I stood on some kind of summit

where there was nothing but silence
and the sound of my own breathing.
A sweetness like clover broke inside me.

I lowered the black barrel, not knowing why.

And considered a bird in the world with both eyes.

He Remembers the First Saturday
of His Backpacker's Trip Abroad

To Casare Pavese

A calm, molten sea at dusk,

and a distant cavalcade of clouds

as the fishing boats drifted in.

And the small waves' sloppy quiet beneath the pier,

the metallic cries of gulls, the drowsy buoy bell,

a hammer's echo from a harbor rooftop,

the kelp in the shallows swaying red and green,

the herring flash in that suavity,

and the sudden whir in the shoreline poplars,

poplars, not maples, the grape leaves stirring

in the tavern trellis, the clouds darkening overhead,

the first plop of rain in the dust at my feet.

Rain pebbled my hotel room's dirty skylight.

On the table, my unfinished letter home,

postcard scenes side-stepping my life, as usual.

I lay down on the double bed

and drifted inside the empty minutes.

The rain ended. I rose in the silence

and hoisted up the bedside window.

Above the harbor, a melon slice of moon.

From an open window, a clatter of plates,

and laughter of men, of women.

I pulled the window down.

I returned to the letter and wept. Wept, not cried.

I still believe this happens to everyone.

Depression

Just by walking I waded in.
The risen moon hung to my left:
a cold medallion.
Just by wading I walked in deep.
And the waters closed over my head.

And I dwelt awhile in the deep
where I could breathe without help
and still resemble myself
though my life had descended toward a November
three-in-the-morning swaying of kelp.

I waded out the way I waded in.
A naive walker, I guess.
And I surfaced into an eggshell day
of sun & wind not knowing how or why.
At least I blinked.

Field Notes

Another splash from the river.
You step through the deep,
luminous day to draw near
the place maple leaves drift down to water
and the blackened, white-snouted Chinook,
Buddha faces by the hundreds
in their fiery masks eddy against the current:
September's ripened fruit aimed upriver.

Another leap-splash.
A twenty pounder hurls itself
against the current,
explodes in a diamond pollen of sunlight
and passes one prone
in the mud beneath a swaying maple,
gills working. A verb subsiding into noun.
Its skyward eye a sunless stone.
The others rest before moving on.

On the Road to Assisi

What we crave is reality.
— Thoreau

He trembles yet still he calls
through the dusk to the quick shadow
sliding along a low, white wall
that brings what sickens him:
the scent of rotting flesh.
He trembles, but he has called.

The shadow stops.

He fears how shallow
his lake of courage might be.
Now come the tears.
Still, he takes a step forward.
And another.

The shadow holds steady.

One more step.
There is no turning back.

A hurricane beats inside his brain.
The shadow remains.
Francis flings his arms around it.
Human flesh, moist and breathing.

In his arms, the shadow remains.

Francis presses his lips
to the cheek of a leper.
And steps back.
Neither man drops his eyes from the other's.
It is the eyes Francis would remember,
the sundered world behind those eyes.

How that gaze into his eyes never faltered.

Henri Rousseau on Trial

> *We are the two great painters of our epoch,*
> *you in the Egyptian style and I in the modern.*
> —— Henri Rousseau to the younger, somewhat
> baffled Picasso.

While Henri looks on from the docket

(So much depends that he wears his blue beret)

his lawyer begins turning some paintings

to the jury and just happens to wonder:

"May we expect the one who painted these

to grasp the meaning of writing bad checks?"

And the crowded room, struck mute,

beholds the strange procession of those things

only a child falling asleep might know.

Wild beasts with a bird of paradise.

A serpent spellbound by a wizard's flute.

A sleeping gypsy, a lion, and a moon.

And Genesis waters. And mysterious zoological species

from a Mexican jungle he's never seen.

Even Red War rides with a naive harm.

The Eifel Tower noodles against blue sky.

And the portraits: yes, we are like bright balloons!

Picture upon picture of celestial candor
born somewhere between kitsch and the Grail.
And each one chiming, despite our underground fears,
that life is ever full of happiness and charm.

The state attorney sounds no objection:
he stares at a duck-billed antelope.
The judge is smiling, his teeth out in the open.
Then the jury, everyone is smiling like those
who suddenly love the whole world around them.
And this is where Henri (provincial customs agent,
a life of deadly dullness, they shall write),
should tip, if he wears it, his customary blue beret.
For surely it's happened: out of clouds white as lambs
has come his guardian angel to intercede.

1891: Arthur Rimbaud at Home Before His Last Journey to Marseilles

Returned to the land of his childhood

without his right leg

(Sometimes he forgot which leg was missing —

the mark of a true poet),

he lay in his shuttered room and sipped poppy tea

while in Paris three hours down the rails

toasts were raised in the advanced cafes

to the "century's greatest poet,"

the late, mysterious Arthur Rimbaud,

vanished into the Abyssinian night.

"Shit on poetry!" is how Rimbaud,

from the battlefield of his bed

reassured his physician,

as if he knew the need to cauterize,

there and then, the future's cafe bohemians

and suburban bacchantes

bound to nail and worship his misunderstood

ghost to the Cross.

And yet, sometimes when the agony
of cancer quieted, the hated mother
off to market and the doting sister
reading or dozing downstairs,
he would sit up and strum the Abyssinian harp
he'd carried back.
Then, his self-confessed cold, wretched heart
would open a crack
as he hummed a naive, haunting tune.

And the good bourgeoisie of Charleville
gathered in the dusk beneath his window
to hear the strumming and strange humming
from the long-lost hometown terror
once proud with lice,
who smoked his clay pipe upside down,
who'd wandered far into the world
off the wonted paths
the good bourgeoisie would stroll home on
shaking their heads,
the alien music fading behind.
Light a candle, then, for the one among them
who doubted, out East, he'd gone mad.

from That Which We Have Named (2008)

Campfire

No politician or puffed chest in sight.

What's left, then?
The Milky Way.
Surf boom and crash.

And a handful of souls
who lean to the coals
crumbling toward ash

like the legendary cities.
Now the stories,
the real stories begin.

Credo

A white sail tacks beneath the thunderhead.
Beach grass rattles at my feet.
The sail slows, shudders, dips and rights itself,
bellying again to go with the wind.

In that distant rudder hand, I know,
there must be no void or empty nave
golden with lawny twilight.
I know how wind and water will braid

to bully and twist a spar, force a curtsy
of white sail. As I grasp the need
to know, not guess, beneath a thunderhead,
how to carve a progress into the wind,

every foot hard-won as a vineyard cliff.
As I know that eyes that long for the windless
light of heaven must, in the end,
reflect the light and shade of earth.

What Men Don't Know They Fear, Exactly

— after Sappho

A summer campground. No red wine. No beer.
Only the immaculate full moon of August
rising above the bonfire.

And the shadows of the women —
their wives, daughters, arise.
And slowly begin to dance.

What Was It?

Was it only the long line of sea
curling to green glass
to boom and shatter white
on the rocks far below
in a rhythm old as Genesis
that made you reach for my hand
in a way that suddenly lacked
all inhibition?

Beside the River

Through the fog
I can hear
the creaking approach
of oarlocks
and the blustering,
in and out,
of two men's voices
as they rehearse
the news they bring.

I stand on shore,
arms folded.
And like all of us,
from all times,
I take a deep breath,
watch and wait
as the river
beneath the fog
moves by like silk.

Redevelopment

The right to let your
rotting dory roped
to an old willow
exist just below the water line
like a not quite abandoned prayer
until kingdom come
seemed inalienable once.

When the Phone Rang Near Midnight

I shed sleep like an old, thick skin to get to it —
an institutional but kindly woman's voice in the American night.
"I'm sorry, but James passed away about an hour ago."

He was ninety. It was expected. Yet I tread frigid water.

Maybe it was the word "James." No one called him that.
It was Jim, mostly. Or Jimmy. Or Jimbo or, long ago, Seamus.
(His grandfather was Irish). Either way, they all added up to
"dad."

And now James? Jesus H. Christ. This really must be serious.

Spring

For the first time
in my fifty-six years
as I walk beneath the immense
weightlessness of spring —
apple blossoms shining
against cornflower blue,
somewhere the small sound of a stream —
I whisper the word "Father"
and it drops like a spent coin
into dark water.

Emily Dickinson

It wasn't her father's heavy Male hand
that stayed her from publishing.
Those who declare otherwise will never
grasp the desire not to be talked about
though the talk might be gold.

Nor the suicide who departs without a note.
Or the one who treasures life enough
to avoid a funeral's orange-carpeted stain
upon the silence. There is a beauty only silence can bear.

Those who think otherwise will never understand
the eagle courage that endures while the world catches up.
Or the one who slips her poems into a drawer.

Seattle Asian Art Museum

In Memory of Steve Kikuchi

Lightly as moths, or scarves, patient
as the seasons, the Japanese women
set up their ikebana displays
for tomorrow's crowds.
Branch. Flower. Shadow. Stillness.
Time and Eternity. Beauty. Death.
These are their materials and meanings.
Words, cracked vessels, cannot hold them.
In silence one pauses, puts back a strand
of long, black hair behind her left ear.

Everything just so.

Two Scenes from the Rodin Room, Palace of the Legion of Honor, San Francisco

Christ and the Magdalene

His splayed arms trace the invisible cross

pregnant within the cross-hatched lava

of an inchoate universe.

Without mirrors, she embraces Him.

Hawk-fierce, she holds nothing back.

All that is required: a bottomless thirst.

That much, and, at last, a gazing up

into a face until the old life blazes

into a sacral pyre.

Prodigal Son

Willing himself, or pressed, despite himself,

almost to his knees,

the pain-plundered face, the flung arms aim

heavenward as if into a drought-ending rain.

He has come home where a father's
forgiveness is the blade that pares
the old life into the river.
It's almost too much to bear.

This is the moment of truth he paid
all those years with false coin to avoid.
Now his swerving dance is done.

The rest of us stand here flat-footed.
Rodin, volcanic mocker, shreds
the gossamer of our days as the sword
of truth runs us through.

On the Crucifix of Unknown Origin in Perpignan Cathedral, France

And when the chin touches the chest, the Catalans say,
— then will come the end of the world.

An existence twisted as a blackberry vine.

A man fated like the rest of us.

A stone face chiseled by the hand of pain.

Spread arms end at the soft, upturned palms

calm as bays, pierced by spikes.

His rib cage: suffering made articulate.

Our eyes can't look away. They slide

to the feet, one topping the other,

positioned *en pointe* for a single spike.

Impoliteness or someone's random hate

did not cause this. Nor the innocence

that attracts wolves.

This is a chess game with the Absolute.

A burnt ember that curls towards the sky.

Chartres Cathedral: The Labyrinth

A large circle, forty-two feet across,
inscribed into flagstone.
Centered there: a small circle
flush with the six petals of the rose,
the celestial city where, when you arrive,
you may look up.

To get there, along the feints
and intestinal twists
of a path barely wide enough
to hold your feet faith must be
the cornerstone. Lack of it
is why you stumble.

Be forewarned. This is a path
far from the cities, the universities.
Here you must depend upon
the rhythm of the rivers, the hills,
the processions of clouds, of sun and rain,
of your most sacred heart.

It's up to you where you place your feet.
Or your knees, like the pilgrims of old.
Out of the common day you might unearth
how much eternity dwells inside you.
Or how a rose might bloom from a humble heart.
Move with cliff-edge care.

And your diurnal thoughts
that dart from tree to tree will slow,
the clenched breath fade
like thorns from the rose
as your slower steps take you
where you have always wanted to be.

You may, of course, mock the path.
You may, of course, step straight as a Roman Road
to the rose from the subdivisions of the heart
and inscribe a perfect line through nature.
Remember, though, the old, winding path remains.
And will remain.

from Coracle (2011)

In October: That Day

And the sun lit the well water
for the last time that year.

A slant wind, warm as April,
rattled the Sunday maple.

In the valley, a grass sea flowing,
the bowed orchard's hard glitter

and the river's bovine placidity
pocked by salmon.

And the dry mountains stood sharp
as broken glass.

A red-tailed hawk drew
a slow circle on a river of air.

In the garden, a Cyclopean sunflower,
worn red roses, a lingering scent of basil.

And the crows, merely themselves,
settled on flamed branches.

And the beholder became the sunlit clarity.
And the heart beat without desire except that life go on.

Facing Panels

I

Wind and rain thrash the grassy field.
Surely God can hear the mice scurry.

II

A hawk tightens its circle above the sunlit field.
I can hear the silence.

July 29, 2006: Off Suquamish

The faraway lines of canoes
move in a mile-long centipede crawl
upon the cloud-dark water.
So ends the journey of the saltwater nations:
Haida, Makah, S'Klallam,
to the Suquamish shore.

There many people will feed them.

The canoes move in the old way
when water was a road, not a moat.
To remember the old way, I make a sunshade of my hands
to block out the steel and glass towers in the distance,
the vertical shimmer of a city
that bears the Suquamish chief's name.

The city from where people will come to take pictures.

I try to keep my eye single, fixed upon the canoes.
Maybe you'll hear it, faint as the silence
in back of silence, a steady, deep-earth chanting.

And maybe your heartbeat begins

to find its proper scansion.

Your portion of eternity.

Old Couple

Says she: "It's a full moon tonight,"
who carries her life in a gunny sack.
Walking beside her, so does he.
"Almost full," he corrects softly as moss.

They part a sea of pigeons in the square
as blue July thrums over the towering city
where their braided being moves like spring rain.
Or two deer sloped to a moonlit lake.

Gerard Manley Hopkins Before Taking Holy Orders: Journal Entry, April 1868

Dover ferry to Ostend on a white-capped sea.

A slow, calm riverboat to Brussels

to catch a steamer down the Rhine.

A stop in Cologne for Sunday Mass.

All the way to Mainz sun-struck poplars

ticked by along the river.

Then to board a train that blew past

peach trees in bloom

before the steep vineyards opened into Basel,

immaculately Swiss Basel

where the full moon lit the empty

nineteenth century streets.

Where, in a high window,

a young woman pushed back her long dark hair,

lit a candle, glanced out not quite long enough,

and was gone.

Tipping Point

Leaves lie in yellow drifts
beside the stream where
the salmon made their run.

The bare orchard's
topmost apples brown
in the biting wind

that shakes the rowanberries
bent to the pond where
the patient stars will come.

The short day hurries on.
And there is something, once again,
that won't return,

as far gone as a leaf's shadow
printed inside a stone,
or a long-ago radio waltz.

What is needed now
was never written down.

Before the First Christmas After My Father Died

A slow lantern
follows the low tide

in the solstice dark
deepened by rain.

The one who bears it
moves, it seems,

with a sure stride
even as the lantern fades.

A Black and White Photograph

The crafted oak door
blond as wheat
bathed in beveled Shaker light
is right in itself
the way it hangs on its hinges
with trust in a universe
that opens into a cool, silent room
like the one you've always hoped
would be there deep
as a well inside your own life
where everything is plumb
for what is next and necessary
and your life, at last,
needs no explaining.

Rome: Michelangelo's Pieta, St. Peter's Basilica

When Zephyr combs a field of wheat it's the wheat in motion we remember, not the ancient name for the wind. To stand before the *Pieta* is to look through theology to an intense actuality in marble. No picture book can prepare one for the real thing.

Her dead son is draped across her lap. Mary's outstretched left hand, palm up in heavenly supplication, articulates a grief only a mother can know. Her right hand helps hold him up.

If Mary stood, she would stand seven feet tall, a grief towering over her son. And she is younger than he is. Her grief is ageless. It stars the basilica's gloaming with an arctic solitude that never ceases to draw a crowd. Even if we didn't know it before, this is what we have traveled to find: a work of human hands that cracks open a door we didn't know was there, delivering us, for a few moments, into a place where we are no longer tourists on earth.

from As We Are Known (2014)

Far and Near

For Jean and Karen

He told of a windblown sea of rye
wrung from a rock field
where roses wreathed a bull's horn.

His Adam's apple moved like reptilian
heartbeat as he glugged another pint.
I was twenty-two and he was old.

"It's fine to speak to strangers
if you have something to say,"
he admonished as the setting sun lit his pint.

That is, as long as I was prepared to listen.
His blade-edged lips continued to spill poetry.
I saw a green, corrugated sea, a blob
of March sun mixed in, and an old-growth island

beneath a crescent moon in the east.
A green and rocky place in a hard wind
where a holy well abided

that had quenched many a nameless thirst.
"Beautiful," I said. "That was really beautiful.
How long did it take you to write it?"

He clapped me a watery-blue Ahab's eye
before he hissed: "Piss on poetry from a proud tower."
It's been forty years since I turned my back on him.

The door opened out into the Irish dusk.
Venus, a magnesium flare, burned small and bright
as a secret vow. Which I've kept.

The Book

Each heart carries the Book of its true life.
Torn pages, a broken binding,
underlined passages, some blacked out,
but the book, flapping in wind and rain
or lying open in a sunlit garden, whispers
faintly as a pigeon's wing-beat across
a sunrise bay: this is the true Book.

We think we can read it through
the glare our own lives make. We think
we can write and read the story we are in
though our story drifts farther away
toward a paid obituary with each
run-of-the-mill swerve over wine
or genial conversation. Few are the words
that don't push away the true.

The Book shadows the shadow our bodies make.
The Book won't sneeze when our flesh turns to dust.
This is the Book, in the end, we cannot read.
This is the Book, from the beginning, that reads us.

Clasped to our breast like a romantic folly,

it follows us into the flames or our graves

with everything that happens to be true.

Father

This is the last poem I will write for you.
This is the last time I'll speak of your fair blue eyes.
Take this hail and farewell for now we are through.
One thing you have taught me: everyone dies.

This is the last time I'll speak of your fair blue eyes.
Never again will my words bring you this near.
You have taught me: everyone dies.
That there is everything, and nothing, to fear.

Never again will my words bring you this near.
Let's clink glasses and go our own way.
So, I have everything, and nothing, to fear.
Our glasses are empty. What more is there to say?

Take this hail and farewell for now we are through.
As if this were the last poem I will write for you.

from the sequence *Fidelities*

Not Quite

"Just one more swim," she whispered from bed.
Now, light as a dove's feather, my mother floats
from my arms that carried her
to this bed of blue water.

My beautiful, cold-water swimmer
cancer-whittled to twig-tree of bone,
you have arrived at the lustrations
of your true home.

Floating on your back you whisper:
"I'm dying in the most beautiful summer ever."
And with an unreturning sigh
shy as the day moon

your sea-green eyes fix on the sky
at the depthless place, and the injured bird inside you
folds its wings. How I wish I could say, my dear,
this is how it happened.

It the Beginning

"You're sure tough," says the ICU nurse.

Says my mother: "Not by choice."

I kiss her warm forehead.

Last night's emergency surgery interrupted the blood clots inching up her right leg, courtesy of the undiagnosed cancer. Now, her lipstick is on, her dark hair spread against the white pillow, regal and beautiful as ever.

Enters a young man, a social worker with a clipboard. "What are your goals during your stay with us?"

Comes that mother's look I know so well. "To learn French," she replies jauntily.

I turn away, afraid to catch her mocking eye. We could always share a joke.

Sympathy

Late June

How cancer threshes
an eighty-seven-year-old
body of flesh as it polishes
the Masque of Death
little need be said.

About the dance of friends
(Some with two left feet,
others with the tread of angels)
around the dying
is the subterranean story of our lives.

"A person in my position
learns interesting things
about human nature,"
my mother offered. I didn't ask
if the news was good.

An unspoken mercy, at least:
no honeyed words arrived

about God's plan.
She kept smarter friends
than that.

It was the corpulent Texas cousin
whom she hardly knew
who won the sweepstakes by phone:
"Forty pounds! I would love
to lose forty pounds!"

Tides

From her sunbathed hospital bed

beside the dining room window she whispers:

"This is the most beautiful summer ever.

I should be swimming."

She gives me that look: "So should you."

"Tide's out," I reply.

"You have no idea."

I turn away to avoid the last glint of mirth in her eye.

I had thought we would always share a joke.

Departure

Her journey is done.
They've black-bagged her body
and wheeled it down the outside stairs
into the Sunday morning sun.

"Zip it just below the chin
so we can see her face," my sister said.
Outside, a few Sunday morning cars go by.
One slows, taking the scene in

before it speeds up when I return the look.
I turn back to her face, still part
of the day in which she died —
the last page of a still-open book.

In the driveway, before they roll her
into the white, unmarked van
my brother leans over, taking his time:
"See you later," he whispers.

My sister and Judith stand at the door's threshold

downstairs, having washed the body.

As I, one more time, kiss her forehead —

two hours and already refrigerator-cold.

The Return

The orchards bow with fruit.

The spawning stream runs rich.

A soft wind brings a rattle to the molting alders.

A few yellow leaves drift with the current,

out of the wind, at last.

The most beautiful summer anyone

can remember has passed.

Now she is part of the beauty.

Shelley

A white sail bellied in the morning breeze.
Through gin-clear water he watched his tall

shadow glide across white sand. Afterwards,
they said he should have left the day before.

Sometimes if you wait, so do storms.
His end is written in the books.

His true end, like all true ends, cannot be written.
How it might have been when he drifted down

his dreamed-of, prismatic depths pushing away
death's hood to see with his eyes that would be pearls

the last poem he would have written.
How, overhead, the impasto green waves slackened

back into gelatinous blue. How that night,
Venus shining in the west, was remembered as serene.

Portland Art Museum

Railroad Tracks Near Acton, 1940
— by Emil Kosa Jr.

A lavender butte for background
protuberant as primal fact.

The European War is far out of sight.

A small road bends and sways
through a brown cutbank.

A row of cross-beamed telephone poles.

One, out of synch, leans left,
held up by its wires —

the right torque and repose

for the kinds of conversations
that will last one more year.

Really Trying to Pray, But

I want the purifying flame to take me
but not get singed.

I hunger for humility
except on an empty stomach.

I pray to be enveloped in the Cloud of Unknowing
but I want to keep my name.

Can't I let go of everything
while holding on just a little?

Even if I jumped from the highest bridge
this is the note I'd write on the way down:

Fall, fall, you already-dead fool.
OK, get ready to swim.

Six Weeks

The doctor says the man swimming with cancer
has maybe a half-dozen weeks, not months.

Which means his eyes will touch the lilacs of May
and the cascades of white hawthorn one more time.

First, he must put down his old Appaloosa.

He steps out the door. His eyes sweep his forefathers'
farm that will fall to his oldest son.

A robin carols, rich as the coming blossoms.
A mossed stone glows in the cloud-light.

The swayback barn still keeps out the rain.

He opens the paddock gate, the 30-30 that put
many a meal on the table cradled over his left arm.

The old horse, slow monolith, moves towards him,
sure as moonrise.

The man's hand strokes the brown, anvil forehead.
He feels the skull.

They stand together in the enclosure beneath the clouds
of March for a little while longer.

from *Departures: Poetry and Prose on the Removal of Bainbridge Island's Japanese Americans After Pearl Harbor* (2019)

Saturday, December 6, 1941: Bainbridge Island, Washington

In memory of Michele Antoncich

Dusk darkens the water's seal-smooth skin.

The old Croatian farmer,

a strong nave of a man built for storms,

rows out upon Eagle Harbor to touch

flame to wick in the harbor light

that guides the ferries in.

With mandarin calm the first stars

come into their own.

Eight miles across the water,

Seattle's modest glow reddens a filament of cloud

where a freight train passes along the waterfront

with a faint, lathe-like thrum.

Wick lit, he admires the first festal lights

shining from the cottages

scattered around the harbor.

He crosses himself, as always,

dips his oars back into the sound of water

and rows for home.

There he will have his own wine to drink,

garnet as arterial blood,

and break his wife's warm bread

to christen the season of lights.

South, above Eagledale's dark firs, a star spills

from the wayside of infinity.

Adieu

After long talk of war and its alarums
approximately 7:55 a.m. Hawaiian time
on a warm, blue Sunday
the bombs fell on Pearl Harbor.
Around 11:25 PST an Associated Press
radio bulletin informed the nation.

How many souls at day's end
secretly gazed upon a beloved face
from that secret place within
and whispered to a world
already being borne into the past:
"I shall miss you."

Remembrance: December 7, 1941

Sometimes monumental events, like the little things, come at us sideways.

A cod-belly gray Sunday, with Christmas vacation only two weeks away. Out riding her bike with a friend, she heard people talking about a war. That is how most people first learned about Pearl Harbor—a glimmer, a gleam. She'd never heard of the place.

Confused, she rode home and told her siblings about the talk of war. They switched on the radio. That afternoon and evening the radio streamed nothing but bad news as Japan advanced in the Far East.

The next day was school, a day in which the U.S. Congress would declare war on Japan. She felt anxious, but the teacher told the class that Japanese Americans were Americans: they had nothing to do with the war. Still, she felt nervous. As the days passed, her anxiety subsided.

For now, the boundary stones of the thinkable stayed put.

Wee Hours

"This is no time to mince words."

So wrote weekly newspaper publisher Walt Woodward in the wee hours after the Date Which Would Live in Infamy. Through the cold, dark morning, Walt and his wife Milly prepared a one-page special edition of the *Bainbridge Review*.

"There are on this Island some 300 members of 50 families whose blood ties lie with a nation which yesterday committed an atrocity against all that was decent." The *Review* warned against "mob hysteria" and "a blind, wild hysterical hatred of all persons who can trace ancestry to Japan.

"The Japanese Americans of ours haven't bombed anybody. In the past, they have sent, along with our boys, their own sons—six of them—into the United States Army."

Digging deeper down, and looking farther ahead: "Let us so live in this trying time that when it is all over loyal Americans can look loyal Americans in the eye..."

Already, up and down the West Coast, hatred stirred in its larval sac. And Walt and Milly Woodward stepped out upon their lonely road together.

The Press

I think it possible that, if Seattle ever does get bombed, you will...see some University of Washington sweaters on the boys doing the bombing.
—Edward R. Murrow

War dines upon our inner dearth.

And so, a whirligig of furies took to the cankered hoof.

Even Edward R. Murrow, journalism's patron saint,

knelt as a footstool for the Perennial Id

to mount the pale horse that leaps

our well-trimmed hedges into ashen pastures

where the fisted heart pumps sulfurous wine

and little children mutter obscenities.

This, too, is a page from the Book of Earth.

From FDR's Pen

February 19: President Franklin Delano Roosevelt signs Executive Order 9066 creating "exclusion zones," the borders of which will be determined.

March 2: Lieutenant General J.L. De Witt issues Public Proclamation No. 1 defining the geography of the West Coast exclusion zones.

Bainbridge Review owners, like many others, think the exclusions include those of German and Italian descent— that this was an equal-opportunity act. "The *Review* is glad it will strike all fairly and without bigotry and without malice," the *Review* states.

Not quite. Japanese Americans are targeted, even as their sons join up to fight. In a later edition: "There are many heartsick people on this island today...The *Review*...and those who think as it does—has lost."

March 24: Soldiers in World War 1 era, tin-pot helmets board the ferry from Seattle to post Civilian Exclusion Order No. 1: "Instructions to All JAPANESE Living on Bainbridge Island." They must be gone by or before Noon, March 30. Six days notice, heralded by the sound of nails driven into wood this Lenten season.

Front Page Editorial

"But we are talking here about 191 AMERICAN CITIZENS!
Where, in the face of their fine record since December 7, in the
face of their rights of citizenship, in the face of their own
relatives being drafted and enlisting in our Army, in the face of
American decency, is there any excuse for this high-handed,
much-too-soon evacuation order?

Departure Eve

Sunday, March 29

Three young breaths plume the dark:
my mother, her little sister, and their friend Mary.
They set out from their safe, Wing Point world
to make their way through the budding woods and orchards
they know by heart with my mother, at sixteen, in the lead.

They come to an old house in a clearing.
The family, including a quiet boy, their schoolmate,
stands on the porch to greet those who've come to say goodbye.
Headlights flash up and down the driveway.
Hugs, whispers, sometimes tears, come and go.

The old grandmother in her rocking chair is steadfast
as a bowsprit. She hands an orange to each visitor.
Oranges that glow in the starless night, just enough to light
the way home for my mother, my aunt and Mary
for the rest of their lives.

Concurrence

The cloud-covered moon is two days short of full.

"Moonlight Cocktail" by Glenn Miller and his Orchestra tops the Billboard charts.

Eleanor Roosevelt, in her March 30 "My Day" newspaper column, will report a "beautiful" day after a quiet walk in the woods at Hyde Park.

The first mass transport of Jews from France arrives by train at Auschwitz-Birkenau.

Life Magazine's March 30 issue is in the mails. Cover story: "Shirley Temple Grows Up."

On Bainbridge Island, the Sabbath bells have long since been quiet. An empty dock waits. Of sleepless nights, no count is taken.

Ticking

Monday Morning March 30

Remember hide-and-go-seek —
that basilica of stopped time as we took
a last look around at our secret place
before a pair of hands juddered the hedge?

They waited, counting the days
from Tuesday to Sunday,
then the Monday morning minutes came
like a moving knife's edge before a big

truck growled in the driveway. A last sweep
of the eyes over the precious rooms
they would never leave. Then
a knocking. And not from the heart.

The Dock

Plum blossoms bitten out against the gray.

Helmets. Bayonets. Rain threatens.

That's not what falls from a few soldier's eyes.

High school has been let out for goodbyes.

My mother and grandmother stand in the crowd.

No one, especially the exiles, know they are California bound.

The nightmare clock has ticked down

to this: the remaining steps to the ferry Kehloken,

the last patch of Island earth beneath their feet.

In Seattle, crowds gather at Marion Street,

waiting to watch the "aliens" marched to the train

for a journey to destination unknown.

Remembrance: Transit

The little girl who overheard talk of Pearl Harbor on December 7 found herself, with her family, at Eagledale dock. She saw the well-wishers who had come to say goodbye. She saw the tears. And then they were marched on board the ferry.

They were marched off in Seattle. She saw the overpass between the First Avenue block and the ferry dock packed with onlookers. An outdoor theater of expectation. The southbound train halted at its final destination the morning of April Fool's Day. From where the train tracks stopped, they boarded buses for a four-hour trip along a winding, high-desert road to Manzanar. They arrived just after noon.

Resistance

The "fortunes of war," when they turned,

brought talk of the Nikkei's return.

Most letter writers to the *Review* wanted them back.

Not all. A man with a crackpot economics book to his name:

"We knew them as neighbors," wrote the No Return Leader,

"as the smiling and inscrutable operators

of truck farms and grocery stores."

Then came his spew of raw racism, those excremental words

ever abiding in unlit cellars.

Then came the public meetings,

the first attended by two hundred. Applause

erupted when one of claimed Indian reservations

a fit precedent for sending their neighbors off.

But the economics author cautioned his allies

against boycotting advertisers in the *Review*.

The *Review* must be kept in business, he declared —

otherwise, who will print our letters to the editor?

And the gods of free speech could only blink.

Return, No Return

Release came. Fewer Japanese Americans
returned to their Northwest and California homes
than those from Bainbridge.

Mob violence broke out in Hood River, Oregon.
Seattle Teamsters prevented Japanese American produce
from reaching public markets.

Assorted West Coast newspapers whipped up
No Return froth. Houses left vacant
stood vandalized, their fields overgrown.

Far fewer No Return voices were raised on Bainbridge.
On Bainbridge there were those who had cared
for abandoned houses, possessions and fields.

The *Review* had done its job. The *Review*
had kept neighbors in touch through the long, dark night.
The No Returners, fists shoved in pockets, got on with life.

The watched-over fields fruited again.

In 2002

Today, on the Eagledale side of Eagle Harbor, a memorial wall commemorates the forced removal of 227 Japanese men, women and children in the place where they boarded the ferry Kehloken for Seattle. The dock is gone.

On the sixtieth anniversary of that day, March 30, 2002, a cloudy Saturday morning, some 500 people gathered on the site of the future wall, then in the planning stages, to remember. The touchstone for the proceedings: *Nidoto Nai Yoni*, "Let it Not Happen Again."

The crowd stood while two-dozen or so Nikkei camp veterans, mostly gray haired, some shoulders bent by the years, sat on folding chairs down front and listened to the proceedings with the patience associated with Japanese culture. A few got up to speak, softly, with restraint.

One man, a dentist and a young child in 1942, was a little more demonstrative: "Down this road we walked in shock. We didn't know where we were going."

A visiting pastor spoke of the soul's brokenness, as if the soul were a limb. "We are here to re-member," he said. Politicians had their say. One recalled Lincoln eyeballing the Other: "I don't like that man. I'll have to get to know him better." Washington's governor, of Chinese ancestry, said, "I don't like the word internment. It was imprisonment."

Heartfelt words were daylighted that morning, and yet they couldn't quite touch the unsunned wells of our lives. Official proceedings have their limits. So does language.

Near the end, something changed.

A tall, dignified man spoke — an Island old-timer of Scandinavian descent who served in the Pacific during the war. He started off telling funny stories about his Japanese American high school pals. That got the crowd laughing. Then he shifted to March 30, 1942, and started to remember how it was in the place where we now stood. His voice fluttered, and then shut down, and he wept.

In the crowd, heads lowered, as did the heads of the Japanese Americans sitting down front. As he struggled to regain himself, heads stayed down. The small waves behind him broke quietly on the mudflats. A robin caroled high in a fir. The silence lasted longer than was comfortable.

This was sufficient.

In the end, a dignitary pulled the covering off a large rock where the head of the old dock stood. Its plaque tells the story of March 30, 1942.

As the sun broke through, the crowd sang "America the Beautiful."

from Suquamish and Other Poems (2019)

Outdoor Interrogation

Once someone asked him:
Where do you live?

Upon an inland sea between
the Cascade and Olympic watersheds.

No, where do you live, exactly?
Oh, you mean exactly.

Where old Steller's Jay shakes a filbert tree in August.
And true friends think before they speak.

Ritual

Slim ballet
of a lone blue iris
in a white vase
centered on the table.
Elegant sundial
for the slant of sunlight
sifting through
the fringed cedar
out the southern window
in this old house
as it does each year
for a week or so
on mid-March afternoons,
delicate as a phrase
from a lost Chopin prelude
you'd give anything
to have stuck
in your head.

Blueberries

"Their lovely modesty,"
she manages to utter. "The Indians ate them.
They knew a thing or two."
So does my older friend on her deathbed,
her well-stocked mind fitted for wandering
the universe in her last days.
A classical musician, a naturalist, a traveler
reduced to a whisper.

"To feel them between thumb
and forefinger in a field in August..."
She closes her eyes. November rain
fills the world outside the window.
Silence, except for the finger-tapping rain.
We stand in an August field
in the radiant world she must vacate.

Of all the things she could speak of:
Rome, Dante, childhood memories
of the white sands of Carmel —
these things she could do

with formal and salty adoration.

But there is only an August field now,

and a blueberry between her fingers.

"I loved them," she whispers.

"And they loved me back."

Query

So, you've brought down
a red-tailed hawk
with a mere twitch
of your trigger finger.

I wonder if
your own return to earth
will exhibit such passionate descent
when your full name is called.

Vincent van Gogh: A Pair of Shoes

— Oil on canvas, 1887

Beaten up.

Beaten down.

Laces akimbo

and two tired tongues

with nothing more

to say than

the face that goes

with these

also wasn't shaped

by the usual roads

of avoidance.

Edouard Manet: Oleander and Clematis in a Vase

— *Oil on canvas, 1882*

Deep in his deathbed

he dabbed

those pink and gray petals

   delicate as Japanese silk

   fragile as French vowels

and placed them into a blue vase.

Petals plucked from time

   to shine outside of time.

Petals to light his way

across the dark waters gathering.

Gwen John: A Corner of the Artist's Room in Paris

— *Oil on canvas, 1907-1909*

The furnishings are spartan:
a wooden table, one chair, an open book on the table,
a window open to the pale sepal of Parisian light.

There is no second chair.
No Gauguin is expected. Gwen's cloistered heartbeat
has thickened the walls between her room and the world.

Her little brother Augustus John,
society portrait artist, King of British Bohemians,
moved through the world like a struck gong.

Once they lived together.
When callers came for her brother, she fled to her room.
She is the better painter, her lionized brother admitted.

"I may never have anything to express,"
Gwen wrote a friend, "except the desire for a more interior life."
September 1939. The curtain rose on yet another war.

Gwen fled to the Normandy coast
where she died alone in her supposed madness quickly,
leaving detailed instructions for the care of her cats.

All this is there, and not there, in the painting
done thirty years before, where the future is a posthumous gaze
any one of us might feel in the last days of summer.

Colmar: After the Rain

In a famous gingerbread town of Alsace
where an old accordionist struck up a waltz
my wife and I danced around fresh puddles
shining from the ancient cobbles.

We followed our feet: one-two-three, one-two-three.
The old accordionist's smile was fey.
I guessed at what he was thinking:
Good tippers, they. Just keep them dancing.

And he did. Even when a Chinese tour group
snapped pictures of our semi-OK box step
in the town my father entered during the War.
He said the name just once when I was a boy: Colmar.

The gingerbread town where my father
had to fight house to house in the coldest weather
Europe had recorded in one-hundred years.
The GI's entered the town by the light of their flares,

a town deemed too historic to shell in advance.
All war is crazy but that made no damn sense,
said my father. And spoke the name of a buddy from Scranton
split by a tracer threading a dark hallway.

A boy whose name I once knew and would forget
by the time my wife and I danced the box step
around fresh puddles seventy years after the War
in the beautiful gingerbread town of Colmar.

from the sequence *Suquamish*

In the Beginning: Where Seattle is Now

The Duwamish River serpentined past longhouses
    to the salt water bay.

Songs came easily as breath beside the green current
    of the salmon-thronged river.

Songs for the spirits
    songs for the seasons
    songs of praise
    and songs of death

In 1851 came the Changers.
    Sooner, not later, the word "reservation" was said.

The Changers, in 1913, turned their gaze to the River:
that which is curved shall be made straight.

In 2001, straight as a Roman road, the River's lower stretch
was declared a Superfund site.

Now the corner offices in downtown's steel and glass towers look down upon the barges and tugs doing the clean-up.

One hundred-fifty years was all it took.
The First People have been here 10,000 years.

Starting from Bainbridge Island

I was born in 1950, five years after the War was won. Five days a week a ferry carried our fathers east to Seattle for their dance of daily bread. Our paved roads were aimed into the future with hardly a bump and little swerving.

The inland sea lapped my green island without undertow.

A short bridge hooked our island westward to the mainland. A mile or so beyond the bridge, down a turn-off road we almost never took, lay Suquamish, burial place of a great chief.

We kept to our island of Rotarians, Little League and weekend spinnakers bellying with the easy wind. Big Daddy Ike protected us from Sputnik. You didn't have to be rich to call the island home. My godfather was a milk truck driver in Seattle.

Twenty years later the new wave of Changers came, who put up turreted manses where torn shoes and chickens once trod the green land. Meanwhile, the strawberry fields dwindled. One newcomer dubbed his llama Aaron Copeland for sophisticated laughs. Then came the slow-down hoedowns and bumper stickers demanding: "Keep Bainbridge Rural!"

And across Agate Pass, a light year away, stood Suquamish, "the place of clear salt water," where stories were told how, fifty years before, salmon leaped so high from the creeks they snapped the fir branches as they fell back to earth.

Suquamish: Chief Seattle's Grave

A few cottages stand among the trees
beside the churchyard. Smoke drifts
from their chimneys into a grisaille
grained with rain.

A white marble cross, flanked by two cedar poles,
marks the great chief's grave,
his feet aimed east.
Clamshells mound the tumulus's base.

Down the knoll white-painted St. Peter Mission,
imprinter of Christ's five wounds
upon the salmon-drumming moon,
stands too tiny for any but candid prayer.

Farther down, the reservation town stands
beside gray waters that touch Seattle
twelve miles southeast, a place of steel and glass towers
named after the white tongue's failure

to utter "Si'ahl" in Lushootseed,

those sounds as far out of reach as the moonlit

talc of salmon bones deep down

nearby Agate Pass.

"And the light shineth in the darkness,

and the darkness comprehended it not,"

said John the Apostle. It may be, in the end,

salvation depends upon right pronunciation.

Chief Seattle's Speech: 1854

Overheard words of uncertain accuracy,

like the words of Christ written down long after.

The past knows more than we do.

The ashes of our ancestors are sacred

and their final resting place is hallowed ground,

while you wander away from the tombs

of your fathers without regret.

Whatever was said, though, came through

sharp as meant nails.

Suquamish, 1959: Burial Place of Chief Seattle

She was just a mom but as Cub Scout den mother
she stood us in the November cold and rain
before a cement cross with clamshells at its base.
I wanted to be home, to be warm and dry,
but I kept in line with the rest of my pack
in its damp simulacrum of reverence.

We all climbed back into the cars that brought us.
I rode with our den mother, who held
open a cemetery gate in the rain.
Who held a gate opening into another world.
I sat in back. Her soft, green eyes
in the rear-view mirror kept to the road.

Months later my parents held a party.
One man's joke about bows and arrows,
fire water and fire crackers triggered such gales
of laughter the ice in their highballs tinkled.
I looked around the room of familiar strangers.
A room where my den mother would never be.

Suquamish: Old Man House

Burned by the Federal government in 1870

Beside Agate Pass where the potlatch hall stood
the salt wind skirls through the emptiness.
A wind that knew a people who'd never met dawn
with their names drawn up on a list by a people
who measured their wealth in columns.
Or answered to men who dreamed of columned manses.

The land is delightful, the country round about
extremely pleasant in appearance.
We saw trees of immense size and calculated for any use.
   — Captain George Vancouver, 1792

Calculations that would employ the words
census, cede, allotment, judicial.
Calculations that would put up white picket fences
to hold back the wind.

Basketball

At eleven we were almost friends.
He lived on the reservation but played

in our Bainbridge Island rec league.
Once his pond-dark eyes looked into mine

then shyly turned away. Once
he whipped me a pass at the bottom

of the key that made me look
better than I was.

We raced down the court side by side.
And spread out to defend the same basket.

Still, once upon a time, side by side.

Once

I paced the northern sands of Bainbridge Island
beside a fast, gray tide already knowing, at fifteen,
indifference was not my fate.

At my back: houses of respectable repute
with their framed, waterfront views.

Across Agate Pass, on the Suquamish side,
a huddle of gray buildings I knew to be a store,
a gas station, two taverns.

Warm rain started, a soft sibilance
falling on both sides of the Pass.

I stood there wondering about the coltish mazes of Providence,
how they dropped me on this side of the Pass
with the wind at my back.

Suquamish Dock

The osprey's pivot
and guillotine
drop

into
a bright confusion
of spray

gives birth
to a slow ascent
on labored wings

and a taloned
flounder flashing
in the Sabbath

morning sun
just beyond the tribal canoe
with six young men rowing hard.

Osprey, flounder,
six young men
acutely there

in the very same world
as the tourists on the dock
snapping photos.

Haiku

from *the road behind* (2003), *contingencies* (2014), *Outside the Garden* (2017)

new calf
apart from the herd:
evening star

cold motel window:
faraway in the dusk
a softball game

Good Friday:
tail lights color
the evening rain

sunset shaft
pierces the cloudbank:
a foal bends to the pond

spring afternoon:

the barber spins me around

towards the mirror

clear-cut:

not even an ironic

butterfly

we men lift

the matriarch's casket:

the lone white cloud

instead

I came here:

wind in the reeds

the last kid picked
running his fastest
to right field

small-town stillness:
yet that headline
in the local paper

the drunk on the dock:
a sweetness unwinds
from his perfect cast

harvest moon:
a distant creaking
of oarlocks

anyway
this is the road
I'm on

the last sun-flash
off the handles
as the coffin sinks

the book I left
in my father's coffin
summer rain

flag-draped coffin
one who set out in a crowd
returns home alone

a standing ovation

for the penniless poet

the short walk to their cars

and the buzzard also rises

my shadow

touches the dunghill

sparrow song

ocean sunset

an old man leaning on his cane

faces it

day after Christmas

sunrise touches

the altar crucifix

sunset

an empty dory

beaches itself

evening star

the outer channel

darkens

one white cloud

drifts over the stubble field

the gate left open

the broom strikes a pebble

which strikes a stone

sunset clouds

the doe
the poachers left
evening star

beaver lodge
of sticks and mud
it begins to snow

a candle-lit window
across the marsh
the first few stars

midnight snow
falls through the hush
it makes

snow falling

upon plum blossoms

time clings to time

ebb tide

the heron's legs

lengthen

cemetery bench
worn smooth
the dogwood in bloom

shooting star
the darkness
down the well

from The Return (2021)

The Return

This is your last return
to the home you never left
on the kind of evening
you'd long imagined.

The first, discreet stars
come into their own.
Venus flares in the west.
The last scraps of birdsong silver
the darkening hedges, as always.

Your parents are dead, of course,
siblings disbursed. The old, swayback house
stands up straight now
and there's a light in the upstairs
bedroom where, once upon a time,
those books before sleep
dreamed you elsewhere.

You stand outside the gate.
You won't knock on the door.

You've hardly returned from Troy.
No Penelope awaits you,
nor faithful dog Argos.

There were blue waters
and there were dark waters.
What happened out there, precisely,
is hard to say.

Here you stand
where old ghosts hover at your elbow.
Where you wear the tattered coat
the future always held out for you.
Where all those things that happened,
and never happened, started out.

Those things you will carry
to the last house.

The Dream

You whispered "Hail Mary" somewhere deep within
as the old priest's nicotine-stained fingers lowered
the immaculate white host of first communion.

Once outside, the sparrow-chirped day stood clean
as sea-washed stone though it was the browned
white hawthorn of late May that held your eye.

You began your search.
You grabbed the rope and hauled your dream —
a half-sunken dory full of stars.

Holy Island: Iona, Scotland

A warm wind whitened the dusk-darkened sea.
Wind that carried the Latin chants of monks.
That teased the summer grass, skirled down
the Street of the Dead, palmed your face and cantered
in the trees as you gazed upon lantern-bright Venus
where it flared over Traigh Ban nam Manach in the north.
Your second day here you stood in your proper dish
of solitude — an American set-piece arrived for a day
who would stay a week.

You watched the cavalcade of sunset clouds,
the sea's darkening ballet. The island, in that dusk,
was a scent of clover after a long sea voyage.
After long estrangement, in the forgotten nave within,
your hands joined to form a candle flame of prayer
flickering in a silence without a name.
This confused you, then.
Even now, you pause to wonder
on the stairs within the self's round tower.

Glimpse

On a yellow stubble plain
where riparian cottonwoods traced
the progress of a slow, blue river,
gleaners in the fields straightened
and waved to the train clicking west.

Came a village of red-tiled roofs,
its bulbous church dome
black as the clouds converging
beyond roofs and woods
to shut an aperture of blue.

Came an empty soccer field
bordered by poplars
flashing in the wind.
And then a small station where she stood
on the crowded platform —

the dark-haired beauty of a face
from a 19th century novel
buried in a veil of deep thought

the train blew past

as your future life hurtled on.

Once

Venus burned just
left of the full moon.
A warm wind
whirred the poplars,
whitened the tide.
And the coppery tang
of loneliness returned
to your life
as the whispers
of two lovers passed.

Thirst

Your canteen rattled empty
well short of the next village
but you stumbled into luck.

Beside the footpath
through a sun-flayed landscape,
a lean man with leathered face

twice your age raked the dust.
You spoke the harsh word for water,
leavened with a question mark.

A sideways glance and nod.
He entered his cottage.
He returned with a jug.

Surely it was the aged mother
who materialized in the door-way,
her toothless maw of a smile

dark as the room behind her.
You drank deep the metallic,
arctic-cold water,

wiped your forearm
quickly over your mouth,
let the lightning headache pass.

Drank deep again.
His wet, robin's-egg-blue eyes
watched you sideways.

Thirst was a duty to be met
born far back in time
well back of Christ.

You returned the jug.
His left hand flickered goodbye.
The right picked up the rake.

It had been served.
Not the dancer but the dance.

Childhood Vacation

Once I glimpsed what the soul might be.
Once there was a white rock on the floor of a lake
no one else in the dory appeared to see.

A dory full of grownups. And me.
I gazed from the cave of some secret ache
and saw through the depths how the soul might be

white as my first communion wafer and free
to live unknown in the world, intact, and to leave
a path through the fields no one needed to see.

I pocketed the rock in my memory,
a north star to steer by for the sake
of helping my life find a way to be.

We think we know the world's story —
its fluky hymns of darkness and daybreak.
But what of the story no one else can see?

That night the wind howled like a banshee.

I stood beside the white-capped lake

with its buried secret of how the soul might be

on a day I glimpsed what no grownup could see.

Home

Maybe the silence of the nothing back home
that helped pack your bags
is the pearl beyond price
you struck out for.

Like so many others you shook
the town's dust from your heels
and figured enough years elsewhere
would point you true north.

You didn't figure, in that far place,
how the silence would detect you.
That it would return like an open, sunlit hand.
That your own hand would reach out.

Not knowing how it found you.

Traveler

At last, you found the other door.
The old locksmith with a rusty key
will let you in. "Just this once," he muttered
before wobbling back into the woods.

You push on the door and step
through empty rooms filled with dusk
and the silence of what has never been said.
One dove-white feather lies upon the hearth.

You step into the kitchen.

On the counter two cracked cruets leak water and wine.
Salt grains the floor. Out of all the paths and bypaths
you have taken or mistaken only one
could have brought you here.

You light the kerosene lamp.
On the back porch, in a soft breeze,
a windchime's sweet, riverine arpeggio
joins the last bird's carol.

Night begins.

Out a broken window:

the gnarled staves of an empty apple tree.

A wafer moon adrift between clouds

lights the unstruck harp of the nothing that is there.

That still awaits your touch.

from *Close Enough*

Kyoto

Who among us has not grown to consider
    what real loss is?

Not loss of grandparents,
    (a grief-cape waved at a bull bearing a padded horn)

or even loss of parents (the horn-pierced heart
    still beats),

but to wonder if we've settled for less
    than the world was ready to give,

or to feel, as Basho did,
    even if it's only for one breath-beat,

what it means to stand in the heart of Kyoto
    longing for Kyoto.

The Author's Photograph in August, Age Five

A sweet gaze locked into the camera's gaze —
still innocent with the shock
of incarnation.

1955: memories forever fixed in black and white.
Even so, I know the stripes on his t-shirt are blue
as the saliva-warm lake behind him.

One day such innocence will grow up to write:
"Just by walking I waded in deep.
And the waters closed over my head."

An underwater forest of too many years
stands between here and there,
though he will find, along the way,

sunlit clearings, green silence of moss,
the silver-shot gleamings of a nameless stream.
And a day will come when he will stop to hear

an unknown bird's liquid carol
along his penumbral path winding
back towards the source of light.

Patience, dear boy.
The path will find the way here
where, at last, I can help you.

Childhood Forest

Far away but close enough to hear my mother's call
I sat in my secret, sunlit place of cedar and salal
in that antebellum year before kindergarten
when my gray, short-haired cat emerged from the brush
with a squirrel clamped in his jaws
to stroll right past me with a lunar stare
into nothingness as the squirrel's mouth
  dripped blood-red berries.

My hushed, urgent calls to my pal,
my bedmate, my friend, did not slow him
from sifting back into the brush
with an indifference that scalded my skin
in a world I had thought secretly loved me,
that left me deeper in the woods that I'd ever been
and those blood-red berries
  shining in the sun.

April 10, 1963

I first heard the word "Jew" said in that certain way at my grandmother's house on April 10, 1963 when I was twelve.

I know the exact date because on the short drive to my grandmother's my mother had the radio on, and there came a news bulletin with a man saying the nuclear submarine Thresher has vanished a few hundred miles east of Boston.

We soon arrived at my grandmother's. She was just back from her first winter in Florida with her second husband, a retired U.S. Navy officer who believed he never got the high rank he felt he deserved.

From the next room I paged through a National Geographic with polar ice and African breasts, but I was really listening to their talk about Florida — the palm trees and warm ocean water.

And then my grandmother's second husband compound-fractured the day: "The damn Jews were everywhere." Then came my mother's "Shhh!" in the way one adult shushes another because tender ears hover.

Goosebumps, and a sudden chill, reminded me of the flesh I wore.

I'd read Anne Frank in school. The good guys, my dad included, had won the War. They couldn't save Anne Frank but they saved the rest of the world. I thought the crow-black shadows had been chased away forever. I thought there would be no more Anne Franks.

On the drive home, the radio off, I didn't say much. The world out the window lay like a sheeted corpse beneath the soft, late afternoon sunlight of April.

I already knew the Thresher had sunk.

Vietnam

A couple of years after high school he came home from Vietnam in a coffin.

A doughy, overweight boy who played no sports, joined no clubs. He nodded off in class instead. His family lived in an old, dingy house on a few tattered acres with their chickens and hogs.

(The place is a manicured gentleman's farm now, with the requisite llama and a pair of golden retrievers).

"I'm sleeping so I don't get tired," he informed one white-knuckled teacher to a squall of teen-aged laughter.

One morning at the school bus stop — this must have been 1965 — he made a running start at the frozen pond and ass-skidded all the way to the other side, accompanied by howls and cheers. He rose in exaggerated slow-motion, made a harlequin bow and doffed an imaginary top hat. He stood there, soaking it all up, the white plumes of his breath vanishing beneath the risen sun.

The school bus neared. The brakes scritched. The yellow door buckled open. And we all boarded for the same destination.

For a little while longer.

Holocaust Denier

As he spoke
to scattered inattention
in the park when I walked past
the faceted interiors
of his green-eyed glance
locked into mine.

And I thought of my cat
hunched on the windowsill
that morning
fused to a towhee flitting
in the laurel on the other side
of the glass.

Puffed cheeks, a guttural chortle.
The green seas of her eyes
dilated black as the spaces
between the stars that frightened
Pascal. I gave her a poke.
She didn't know me.

A Village in Southern France

...the trip is worth it only if the river's
source is flowing.
— from a well-known guidebook

Upon dusty river-rock

mottled shade from a plane tree

flickers with water's fluency.

Upstream the famous fountain is dry.

This lyrical tableau of shade and stone

is not what tourists come for.

So, you wait with the others

for the tour bus to pull up

and point for better things.

The bus is late. Across the lane

there's a small stone chapel:

disused, scabrous,

a ninth century footnote to the town.

You open the oak door

and step into the darkness.

A few apertures of light reveal
a bare stone altar,
a worn keeling place.

Light that carries
an unbroken thread.
As it was. As it is.

At My Father's Old Battlefield: Jebsheim, France

My father never talked
about the War.

Sometimes the steep silence
    of an abandoned well
    swallowed him

and his blue eyes stared off
    into nowhere's
    somewhere.

An hour after his funeral my mother
  said to me
    he cried just once
    in his sleep
    and not like a little boy, either.

In May

Purple wisteria
and a red rhododendron
color a lush green world
in thin afternoon rain.

A brown horse steps
over the far field
with the slow fluency
of a mind at peace.

Rain patters the new leaves.
Rain falls through an archaic memory
not your own. Someone you
would recognize, and would recognize you,
stood here in another century.

And will again.

Close Enough

*I hold this to be the highest task of a bond between two people: that each should
stand guard over the solitude of the other.*
— Rilke

Close, let's not come closer.
There. Close enough.

To keep it like this —
our two-step to the music

only we can hear. Close enough to warm
myself beside your beauty.

Close enough that I may give you
everything you need.

And far apart enough we may never utter
"I know what you're thinking"

across the hairline crack between us —
our precious, rose-petalled moat.

Family Reunion Picnic

Domine miserere nobis

You gaze upon the angelic precision of their sunlit faces,
    the familiar become dear.

Their choric voices and laughter weave a hymn
    you half-heard once drifting from a hill.

Now you understand: this is what you wanted.
    Those years of parched seeking lie far behind.

A white wafer moon floats high overhead.
    A warm breeze flows through the shoreline maples

and moves a lock of your baby grandson's sandy hair.
    The swimming tide is almost in.

There is still time for second helpings.
    Buoyed by tenderness, you rise into the air

to gaze down upon the mother of your wife.
    You call her name. Her face turns into the radiance.

And you ask: "Do you want a little more pie?"
Though "Dost thou" is what you mean.

At Last, the Sea

You ask me, stranger, what route I took
to arrive at the sea's steady interrogation.
I tell you almost anything
and leave out everything
about those I love.

When you say the windy blue sea
is magnificent I say nothing.
I rest my eye, instead, on the taut silence
of a blue flower in the sedge
moving in the sun.

About the Author

Mike Dillon lives in Indianola, Washington, a small town on the Salish Sea northwest of Seattle, from where he writes poetry, essays and occasional book reviews. The former publisher of a group of community newspapers in Seattle, he is the author of six books of poetry, two poetry chapbooks, and three books of haiku. His essays have appeared in *Literary Hub, Kyoto Journal, Rain Taxi, The Galway Review, Northwest Asian Weekly*, and other venues in this country and abroad. Among his journalism awards is a first place from the Society of Professional Journalists for a three-part series on sex abuse. He is also editor of *Notes from the Garden: Creating a Pacific Northwest Sanctuary*, by Madeleine Wilde. Several of his haiku were included in *Haiku in English: The First Hundred Years*, from W.W. Norton (2013).

About the Press

Unsolicited Press is based out of Portland, Oregon and focuses on the works of the unsung and underrepresented. As a womxn-owned, all-volunteer small publisher that doesn't worry about profits as much as championing exceptional literature, we have the privilege of partnering with authors skirting the fringes of the lit world. We've worked with emerging and award-winning authors such as Shann Ray, Amy Shimshon-Santo, Brook Bhagat, Kris Amos, and John W. Bateman.

Learn more at unsolicitedpress.com. Find us on twitter and instagram

www.ingramcontent.com/pod-product-compliance
Lightning Source LLC
Chambersburg PA
CBHW031509120626
46545CB00005B/1809